Primary

Professional

Development

Circles of Friends

Colin Newton and Derek Wilson

Folens
Publishers

186202359X

Acknowledgements

Our joint thanks go to each of our families for all the time out that this book has meant.

Our thanks also go to:
- Gill Taylor who shared in the early development of this work
- Gerv Leyden for his meticulous reading of an earlier draft of this book
- Jackie Dearden who contributed the Circle of Friends story on p.38 – a courageous piece of work.

Many other people have encouraged and supported us in carrying out and writing about Circles of Friends. We won't name them all here – they know who they are. Finally our thanks to all the children and teachers we have worked with, for letting us into their classrooms, trusting the ideas and engaging so honestly in the process. They did the real work.

This book is dedicated to
Jack Pearpoint and Marsha Forest

Editor: Karen Westall
Illustrations: Eric Jones

Layout artist: Patricia Hollingsworth
Cover design: Ed Gallagher
Cover image: 'Flemish Fair' by Pieter Brueghel the Younger

© 1999 Folens Limited, on behalf of the authors.

Every effort has been made to contact copyright holders of material used in this book. If any have been overlooked, we will be pleased to make any necessary arrangements.

British Library Cataloguing in Publication Data. A catalogue record for this book is available from the British Library.

First published 1999 by Folens Limited, Dunstable and Dublin.
Folens Limited, Albert House, Apex Business Centre, Boscombe Road, Dunstable, LU5 4RL, England.
Reprinted 2000 (twice).

ISBN 1 86202 359-X

Contents

Introduction and key themes

'In an intact group the pool of shared understandings is like a shared bank account of the group wealth ... Since it is spiritual or psychological wealth, it does not diminish by being spent. Rather, the more lavishly it is circulated, the greater inner wealth and security each single member feels to have.'

Ted Hughes, *Winter Pollen – Occasional Prose* (Faber and Faber, 1994)

What is this book about?

This book describes an approach to enhancing the inclusion, in a mainstream setting, of any young person (known as 'the focus child'), who is experiencing difficulties in school because of a disability, a personal crisis or his or her challenging behaviour towards others. The Circles of Friends approach works by mobilising the young person's peers to provide support and engage in problem-solving with the person in difficulty. Circles of Friends is *not* the same as 'circle time' but many of the skills and techniques used by teachers in 'circle time' can be used to support the Circles of Friends process.

Who is this book for? Our focus is on the people we are asked to work with, as educational psychologists, the children and young people who are labelled and marginalised in various ways and the people who are paid to teach and provide for them. If you are a special educational needs coordinator, a form tutor, a primary class teacher, a youth worker, a support assistant and you are concerned about the isolation of young people you know with a disability or difference, this is the book for you. It is not about any one label or disability. Ultimately, it is a book for everyone because at some time in our lives, all of us are likely to have needs that are not typical.

Aims of this book

✔ To provide a highly accessible resource that is both practical and meaningful.

✔ For users of this resource to be able to set up Circles of Friends feeling they have sufficient support and guidance.

✔ To inspire and encourage interest in creative approaches to the involvement of children in the inclusion of vulnerable and challenging peers.

✔ To provide a tool that can reverse pressures to exclude and segregate an individual from his or her school community.

✔ To strengthen the processes which help to create and maintain school communities of acceptance to which *all* children truly belong.

What differences will it make?

We hope that the successful use of this resource will lead to the following outcomes:

✔ Disabled and challenging pupils will be successfully included in mainstream schools.

✔ Headteachers, teachers, SENCOs, parents and support assistants will feel they have an approach which actually works; increasing friendship opportunities, helping individuals to belong and decreasing behaviour difficulties.

✔ Pupils will feel valued and involved in the support of other pupils that they know are finding school life difficult. They will have become allies in the support of their peers and will feel safer as a result, knowing that they too one day may need such support in their own lives.

✔ Other creative developments in peer counselling, mentoring, mediation and circle time will emerge.

✔ Deeper insight and understanding of disability issues, emotional and behavioural needs and the possibilities of change will develop.

✔ There will be a greater understanding of the need for peer support and teaming by teachers and other professionals.

✔ Reflection and discussion on the themes of inclusion, circles of support for adults, peer involvement and friendship will take place.

Values base

This is not just a 'how to' book, although it will give you all the information you need to begin the Circles of Friends process around an individual in your school. It offers an invitation to consider the values that inform your work with young people and to spend time considering why we do what we do and where we are heading with our work in schools. This section makes explicit the values that underlie Circles of Friends work. The values we advocate are those of full inclusion for all; the belief that there is no social justice until each belongs and has an equal place in our schools and communities. But having said this, we must also say: 'We do not yet know how to bring this state of affairs into being.'

This fact is put clearly by Herb Lovett, an American clinical psychologist and writer on inclusive and person-centred planning in *Learning to Listen* (Jessica Kingsley, 1996, p.8):

> '... the idea of a completely inclusive community in which everyone belongs is far more radical than it first appears. In the abstract, many people subscribe to the notion of an inclusive community whose criterion for belonging is that you have to be breathing. In practical fact, however, most of us draw lines somewhere. Notice also that where the line was confidently drawn can in a short time become indefensible and unjust. It is easy to forget that as recently as 1973 pupils with IQs of less than 50 were regarded as ineducable and therefore excluded from the school system in the UK. Inclusive thinking is not easy.'

Independence and *inter*dependence

Most of us have grown up in a culture which has taught us that competition is a good thing and that independence is a virtue to strive for. We have been taught that those who are unable to 'win' or be independent have something wrong with them and need fixing by experts. This is a 'top down' model of society and has produced a hierarchy in which there are those who know best and those who are deemed to know least. Little wonder that it is hard for us to envision what true collaboration and cooperation might look like. We are also aware of the paradox that is implicit in saying this – after all, this book was written by individuals who, as educational psychologists, are key players in the hierarchy we are describing as part of the problem! It follows from this that we are the ones who are likely to have most to learn.

The quote from Ted Hughes which starts this chapter is a reminder of the difference between 'spiritual or psychological wealth' and monetary or material wealth. The value of material wealth lies in keeping as much of it as you can for yourself, whereas spiritual wealth is enhanced in value only to the extent it is shared with others. Intact groups will include a diversity of voices and there will be some present who do not use language to express their awareness of the world. At the other end of the life cycle many of the oldest members of our families live a separate existence in nursing and retirement homes. Such forms of exclusion limit our ability to generate and circulate spiritual wealth and experience.

Signing for inclusion

This illustration of the value of diversity in everyday settings was provided by an Infant teacher who is successfully including a pupil with Down's Syndrome in her class. This child communicates by Makaton signing and the class as a whole is learning to use these signs. They are active and enthusiastic in encouraging their classmate to use them also.

The benefits to the disabled pupil are plain. However, there is another pupil in this class who benefits from signs being in everyday use by the group. She is a girl with a profoundly deaf mother and she is bilingual in British Sign Language and in spoken English. Before the arrival of the child with Down's Syndrome, she had felt embarrassed by her untypical signing proficiency and reluctant to admit to having this skill or to share it with others. Since the arrival of another child using signing (the most important thing about the child with Down's Syndrome, in her eyes), she has lost this uneasiness and is happy to share her ability and become a kind of dictionary of sign expertise. In a very real sense, she has experienced 'interdependence'.

Tales of inclusion

' I can't myself raise the winds that might blow us into a better world. But I can at least put up the sail, so that when the wind comes I can catch it.'

E. F. Schumacher, author of *Small is Beautiful.*

Despite our professed ignorance of exactly what we are heading towards and how we might get there, we are able to bring you some 'tales of inclusion' as signposts on the journey and some glimpses of the bigger picture. We can say something about *inter*dependence and tell stories about how everyone benefits when we try to include. It is important that these stories are told because they are an antidote to so much of what is usually written about difference and disability, and because we know that there are many more such stories waiting to be told.

Unless you are able to subscribe to these values and beliefs at some level, 'Circles of Friends' will be just another name for a bit of imposed social engineering where those in power decide what is best for those who are marginalised.

Lessons we are learning

The Circles of Friends process takes a wider look at the relationships in a person's life. As we have looked at this bigger picture, it has become apparent that our usual professional perspective on those relationships has been one dimensional. We have focused on the child or young person solely as someone with special needs who must access the curriculum. But this child is also a son or daughter, a grandchild, possibly someone's brother or sister, a cousin, a next-door neighbour and so on. If we extend this network to include people who potentially share the same interests as the child in question (who love the same pop group, support the same football team, like the same kinds of pets) then we can begin to see that many perspectives on the child are available if only we look widely enough.

Circles of relationships

Here we take a wider look at relationships. In this model, these are seen as being at four different levels of closeness to the person at the centre of the concentric circles. (This account is based on the work of Jack Pearpoint, Marsha Forest and Judith Snow.)

Circle One: The Circle of Intimacy. This is made up of those who are our **ANCHORS** – the people who are closest to us and whom we could not imagine living without. They will typically be members of our immediate family but not invariably so. Younger children may include their pets, especially if they talk and tell secrets to them.

Circle Two: The Circle of Friendship. This consists of those who are our **ALLIES** – the people who are friends or close relatives but who did not quite make it into Circle One. These are people we would confide in and would expect to be on our side and stand up for us in a difficult time. They are key to our psychological life support systems and if our Circle Two is sparsely populated, we are prone to feelings of isolation, anger and depression.

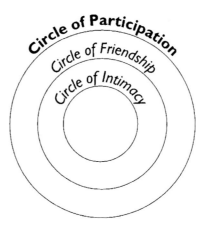

Circle Three: The Circle of Participation. This is made up of our **ASSOCIATES** – the people we are involved with because we see them regularly in school classes, at clubs, organisations, in church and so on. These are the people an individual 'hangs around' with; they come and go and may not always be people we see very often.

Circle Three is typically the circle with the largest number of individuals within it. Some individuals who later figure in Circles One and Two will often have been encountered first within Circle Three. 'We met at Dance Class and were married six months later' is a common progression of relationships. Circle Three is the seed bed for close future relationships and, as we will go on to describe in later chapters, it is the members of Circle Three that provide us with the key participants in a Circle of Friends.

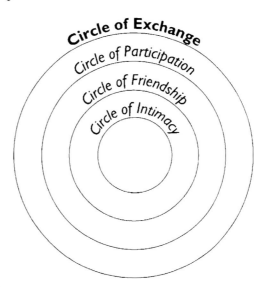

Circle Four: The Circle of Exchange. This consists of people who are **PAID** to be in our lives – doctors, teachers, dentists, social workers, therapists, hairdressers, car mechanics and the like. They are paid by us or our caregivers to provide us with services. Children with disabilities and those in care will tend to have higher than usual numbers of people in Circle Four and this skewing of relationships is a serious barrier to their participation in ordinary community activity.

There is a taboo in Western society that discourages the people who make up this circle from moving any closer in relationship to the person at the centre. Sometimes known as maintaining 'professional distance', the result is that the individuals in this circle are unlikely to become close friends or allies of the focus person. The individuals in this circle also have their own agenda as far as the focus person is concerned and it may not always be the agenda he or she would have chosen. Appointment times, caseload management, agency policies, resource availability and promotion prospects set the terms of the relationship with the focus person.

In Chapter 3, we will describe how this picture of relationship circles can be used in the school situation to begin the process of forming a Circle of Friends.

Circles of support for life

Friends and family: past, present and future ... Some of the most important people in our lives are no longer present with us on a day-to-day basis. They may live a long way away, rarely be seen or indeed may be dead. Present or absent friends and family members continue to play a critical support role in our lives and act as anchors for us as we take risks in our daily lives. They build our self-esteem and are constant internal reference points. These reference points can guide or they can limit, disturb or distort our experiences. Past experience of abuse, loss, separation or rejection may haunt our waking lives and unconscious fears. We may rerun old videos of past relationships in which key people cross in front of our internal eyes and powerful emotions are played out. Still images in sepia, grainy icons of the past, may be current reference points within our circle of living and dead supporters and friends.

Our circles of support change over time. Today they may appear extremely full, while tomorrow we can feel terribly alone and exposed, experiencing loss, isolation, anxieties or depression. This perspective, although focused primarily on children, provides lessons for us all. We all need friends, allies and associates to surround and support us through life. Our families, whilst important, will never be entirely sufficient if we are to reach out and extend our human potential and experience.

Background

Why Circles of Friends?

Circles of Friends is an exciting, fresh approach to meeting challenging individual needs in ordinary mainstream settings such as local schools. The approach promotes the inclusion of individuals who face the greatest risk of rejection or isolation from the community in which they live because of their disability, behaviour or difference.

Why now?

Schools, in the last ten years, have faced unprecedented changes and stress and these usually accepting community settings have become, at times, places of rejection and isolation. Innovation overload, significant changes to working traditions, increased autonomy for the individual school and new management approaches have combined with dramatic changes to the way in which schools are financed, measured and held accountable for standards and improvement. One of the unintended consequences of Government legislation in the past decade has been the increasing marginalisation of vulnerable groups. This process has been accelerated by a developing culture of competition between schools. All these factors combine to undermine the confidence and tolerance of many ordinary schools and their staff to make provision for those with awkward needs. (Newton and Tarrant, 1992.)

The need to review methods and approaches that aim to support and include the most vulnerable in our schools has never been greater. The facts of permanent exclusions running at record numbers (official figures from the DfEE for 1995–6 showed a total of 12,500 pupils permanently excluded from English schools – a jump of 13% on the previous year – and in 1996–7, there was a further increase to 13,500) and of increasing pressure to segregate children with challenging behaviour or disabilities are clear for all to see.

Teachers across the world are seeking new ideas to help them solve what appear to be increasingly challenging demands. Governments, too, are calling for advice on ways of increasing inclusion and the recent Green Paper, *Excellence for All Children* (DfEE, 1997) highlights this as a key target for schools to achieve. Yet we lack the practical tools to help teachers support the inclusion of disabled children and to tackle in a meaningful way the challenging behaviour of disturbed and disturbing individuals.

A Circle of Friends provides a powerful way of tackling severe emotional and behavioural difficulties. These difficulties, of increasing concern to educators across the UK, appear to be exacerbated by the within-school factors mentioned above, and major changes within society.

Teachers are therefore keen to adopt approaches which actually bring about change effectively and with relatively minimal adult resource implications.

Inclusion

'All means all!'

There is a growing international movement advocating the basic human entitlement to inclusion in ordinary, everyday community activities including education. There are increasing examples of full inclusion in mainstream education across the world: schools are achieving inclusion of the full range of disabilities and behaviours in ordinary school settings, diverting resources from previously existing special schools and units. Parents of children with disabilities are increasingly demanding mainstream placement for their sons or daughters. Inclusion is the legitimate goal for all children for the following key reasons:

A human right

All children share the same basic human right to ordinary mainstream education. Children are no longer segregated by ethnic origin and yet they are by disability. They do not need to be protected from one another, nor should they be devalued or discriminated against because of their disability or behaviour.

The research evidence

Pupils with difficulties develop a wider range of competencies in the key areas of cognitive, academic, language and social development when their education takes place in a mainstream setting. More than this, there are benefits for all pupils educated in an inclusive school.

A meaningful life

It is essential to take the 'long view' when deciding what is the best education for children and young people labelled disabled. Children with disabilities are more likely to find acceptance and to form meaningful relationships and friendships if educated in ordinary community settings from the start. Continued segregation only teaches mainstream children to be fearful and breeds prejudice out of ignorance.

These points have been summarised concisely and clearly:

> 'Inclusive education is a human right, it is good education and it makes good social sense.' (Centre for Studies on Inclusive Education, 1998)

This vision of inclusion has led to the need for real and meaningful approaches and tools. Circles of Friends have been used in parts of North America and Canada for a number of years to promote the acceptance of pupils with disabilities in mainstream schools.

Within the North American work, the Circles of Friends approach is used as one means of normalising the life experiences of disabled pupils who are recognised as vulnerable to isolation from the ordinary pattern of extended relationships and friendships. This isolation is associated with a system of segregated schooling where pupils' opportunities to know and be known by the wider peer group in their community are limited by their institutional and often geographical separation on the basis of disability.

What Circles of Friends *is*

Circles of Friends (sometimes known as a 'circle of support') is a **tool for inclusion**. It works by creating the intention to build relationships around the individuals who are vulnerable to exclusion because of their disability, difference or because they face a crisis in their lives. It is a way of building a community that recognises the central importance of relationships and community connections in *all* our lives – for our psychological well-being and for our physical health and resilience. This is the starting point for the work.

No complex psychological theories are necessary. The message is a simple one – relationships are what matter most, whatever labels we have been given, however awkward our needs. There is no cut-off point beyond which someone does not 'qualify' to be included and therefore no one for whom a Circle of Friends could not be built. This is not to say that the community knows how to include everyone – clearly it does not. Too often, acceptance of individual pupils is conditional on their behaviour changing before they are deemed to belong. When attempting to include by building a circle, what changes first is the behaviour of those around the focus person – the person who is at the centre of the circle.

Circles of Friends is not, of course, the only intervention that involves peers to provide support. The 1990s have seen a rapid growth in literature dealing with peer tutoring and mentoring, with peer mediation and conflict resolution schemes, and with peer counselling, particularly as a means of countering bullying in schools. What these approaches have in common is a sharing of responsibility between staff and young people for solving a range of issues that confront every school.

Keep taking the relationships

Research evidence for the importance of a wide circle of relationships in maintaining not just our psychological well-being but also our physical health and resilience continues to accumulate ...

A study monitored 276 healthy men and women between the ages of 18 and 55. They were asked to list up to 12 types of social relationship they were involved in: parent, son, employee, in-law, club member, friend, neighbour and so on. The sample was controlled for factors such as smoking and drinking habits, diets, sleep habits and a range of other variables related to overall health. Each person in the study was then exposed to the common cold virus in laboratory conditions. Sixty-two per cent of those with three or fewer relationships got colds as against only 35% of those with six or more kinds. Why this should be is not known but the evidence is clear – if you want fewer colds, build yourself a wide set of relationships.

What Circles of Friends *is not*

✔ Circles of Friends is not a new approach to the treatment of any kind of disability or emotional and behavioural difficulty.

✔ It is not yet another attempt to look inside the child and diagnose what is missing or deficient. Viewing people's distress and difficulties and the social context in which they are expressed from the medical perspective alone is seldom likely to be the best way of generating solutions. What we will usually end up with is a list of hypothetical deficits, a clutch of possible labels, a feeling of despair and a lack of a clear way forward.

✔ Circles of Friends is not a behaviourist approach to changing someone. It is at the opposite end of the continuum of interventions from an approach such as 'assertive discipline'.

✔ Circles of Friends is not about seeing the child in isolation from his or her peer group: all teachers are aware of 'vicious circles' of peer interaction that can grow round individuals whose behaviour is challenging to others.

✔ It is not about rewarding or punishing surface behaviours. Circles is about looking deeper, looking behind the behaviour and finding the person. It does not involve looking for deficits in people and attempting to 'fix' them.

✔ Circles of Friends is not therefore something experts arrange for someone else. It is about all our lives. We all know about those times when our own circles of friends have been thinly populated for various reasons and about how this made us feel. All of us have had experience of being 'outsiders' at one time or another, of not belonging or of being excluded and that is a reminder that we all have much more in common than we may realise – whatever our difficulties or differences.

The role of pupil culture

> ' ... more than any other factor, pupils nominated relations with peers as a cause for both truancy and disruption ...'
>
> *Talking Back – Pupil Views on Disaffection* (NFER, 1996)

The fact that there is a culture of values and beliefs existing amongst pupils in every school that is separate from what is promoted by staff as the official culture of the school is widely known but little recognised in any of our planning or policy-making. Pupil culture takes some of its identity from the fact that, as a group, pupils are relatively disempowered within their institutions and typically have little say in key decisions. Obviously, pupil culture grows in its complexity and influence as young people progress through the system. In this time, the voice of pupil culture progressively diverges from that of the official culture. As it diverges it becomes increasingly powerful and likely to have a say in whether the 'solutions' to school problems proposed by the official culture are likely to have a chance of success. Consider the following episode.

A solution from pupils

A Year 5 pupil, labelled as a child with autism and attending a mainstream primary is regularly involved in fights at playtimes. It is clear to staff that he is finding it difficult to distinguish between 'playfighting' and genuinely aggressive approaches from others and is responding to every advance with real and retaliatory violence. His confusion is also apparent to the Circle of Friends that the school has built around him. On their initiative, they decide that the only way forward is a schoolwide ban on playfighting. They therefore talk to a school assembly about their reasons for the ban and are careful to stress that the focus child is not the only person who finds playfighting hard to handle. Their plea is successful and playfighting steadily decreases during breaktimes. This scenario makes the point that some solutions are only within the gift of the peer group. If the 'ban' on playfighting had been imposed from above and become an addition to the official rules, the chances of it being complied with as readily would have been much reduced.

Pupil culture's interpretation of school 'rules'

This was made plain to Derek during an open evening for parents at the secondary school attended by one of his daughters. A typical city school, it has its code of conduct for pupils displayed on a poster in every classroom. One of its statements is a reminder to pupils that: 'We work as hard as we can at all times.' When Derek asked his daughter if this was really the case, she replied 'No, you do just enough work to make them think you are working as hard as you can.'

This is the authentic voice of pupil culture and its importance is that it also has a perspective on the individual focus child. One of the most encouraging things that creating circles illustrates is that the picture of the focus child that emerges, when one asks his or her peers, is invariably richer and more balanced than that typically provided by the adults paid to be in that child's life. All we needed to do was ask.

Light on additional resources

The key resources needed to create a Circle of Friends are other pupils. If the focus child is a member of a mainstream school, these key resources are already and always there. This may seem like stating the obvious, but the fact is that this resource has been almost wholly overlooked when schools and outside agencies have tried to meet the special needs of individuals. Indeed, the message to other pupils when one of their group is behaving in hard to understand ways is usually: 'Ignore it – it doesn't concern you … ' Whole chapters of Behaviour Management books for teachers are given over to the act of ignoring and teaching the class to do so also. Of course, the other children don't ignore it. They form their own theories about what is troubling the child being ignored and, somewhere along the line, they run the risk of internalising the message that if you are in distress and can't cope, you will be ignored. The Circle of Friends works by travelling in the opposite direction to 'ignoring'. It notices. The other children are invited to give their views and check out their theories. With this starting point, the focus child's peers are often able to come up with successful solutions to a problem situation or an unmet need, if we only ask them and provide support in achieving it.

Our personal experience

Origins

Although no one writer or researcher created Circles of Friends, the approaches described in this book have been strongly influenced by the work of Jack Pearpoint and Marsha Forest of The Centre for Integrated Education and Community in Toronto, Canada. Through their work, we learned of those parts of North America where there are fully inclusive school systems and no separate special provision, and of the tools that had been used to achieve this. We learned of the 'Communitas' group in Connecticut and its sister organisation in the UK – the Bristol-based 'Circles Network'. These two organisations give an international lead in the use of circles of support as a tool to promote the inclusion of people with disabilities.

Risk taking

We have found that setting up Circles of Friends in schools has been a rich and exciting venture. We have also found that the work carries its own risks. The approach is relatively new in the UK and we were working with some of the most challenging individual pupils in stressed school settings. The work invites teachers to adopt a particular role. The first risk we faced was trusting the teacher to work effectively with the Circle of Friends that we had initiated. The role of group facilitator ought not to be too unfamiliar, but we have found that some teachers find the gear change from large group teaching to small group work demanding. Others who are very familiar with personal and social development activities have found very little difficulty in running circles effectively.

A more personal and at times very challenging risk has been the exposure of ourselves to work with whole classes of pupils and small circles. Educational psychologists have a background in teaching, but do not have, as part of their role, ongoing experience of class teaching or small group work with pupils. We therefore found facing a large group of children stressful and risky. We risked the situation becoming chaotic, denting our professional reputations within schools as a result, and ultimately letting the focus pupil down.

Rewards

In the event, we were rewarded in many unexpected ways. One of the simplest but most powerful was the way in which pupils would run and greet us when entering the school. This is not a typical experience for a visiting educational psychologist whose usual work is discreet, individual pupil-focused and mainly involves discussions with staff and parents.

The risks we had taken to set up Circles of Friends encouraged us to take further risks in our communications about this work to others in the educational world. We took the risk of talking more in the first person and telling our own stories. Doing this allowed us to be ourselves, to be honest as we expected others to be. The following cameo aims to bring alive what this can mean. It summarises an e-mail sent to a national forum for special needs coordinators in mainstream schools, other special educators and psychologists, which was trying to reach out to the people behind the professional roles.

Beautiful moments

'In the course of work as an educational psychologist increasingly tuning in to the goal of full inclusion, I am beginning to notice beautiful moments in the everyday course of my work ... I wonder if anyone else shares these experiences in such a time of horrendous rejection, segregation and exclusion?

These moments have increased since I have been involved in creating Circles of Friends around vulnerable and challenging individuals and become increasingly aware of the importance of a child's natural community, their peer group and contributions. Take two recent moments ...

✔ Ian, a 15-year-old with no spoken language and cerebral palsy, is adored by his two-year-old sister and plays with his five-month-old baby sister. During a transition plan meeting at a special school ... he beams when she accepts the furry toy he offers ... This is the first time his mum has been in the school for eight years.

✔ Bill, the head teacher, warmly offers a part-time placement for Jenny, a girl of seven with no words but a lot of screaming and severe learning difficulties ... He gives her a school sweatshirt, so that she will know when she puts it on that this is the day for her attendance at the mainstream local school, and talks to her sister about what will happen ... No big fight, no mixed messages ... acceptance and welcome.

Small moments, nothing special perhaps, and yet beautiful in their own way and in potent contrast to so much of the day-to-day grind and battles of work in the special needs world. Has anyone else caught a moment to share?' Replies flowed in and included:

✔ 'If the question was "Am I crazy?" the answer is "It depends". It depends whose criteria we use. By regular measures ... clearly you have lost it ... have given up your personal professional distance. However, according to some of us – congratulations. Now we are all listening. Now we can begin to learn. And incidentally – it's a better way to live.'

✔ Kyra began to speak of her father's terminal cancer. Her mother is alcoholic and Kyra can be a 'little spinning top'. When she mentioned that she finds it hard to go and stay with her dad in case he dies while she is there, Laura moved across the circle, put her arm around Kyra and said 'My Nan died'. Laura held Kyra while she cried.

✔ Matthew refused to draw a Santa on his card. 'I can't do them,' he crossly stated. This went on for 20 minutes with many, many tears. Encouraged, and left on his own, he eventually held up a drawing. 'I like the way you've drawn him fat and jolly', I interjected. Matthew beamed from ear to ear. Kerri started to get cross ... 'I can't draw Santas', and Matthew said 'I'll do it for you. I can'.'

No doubt you will be able to relate to the beautiful moments of your own work with children and also will be aware of the risks you might need to take if you are to begin using Circles of Friends in your own school setting. Only you will be aware of the sensitivities of your particular circumstances along with your own professional and personal skills and experiences. If these include anxieties and vulnerabilities, read on, we are with you.

Chapter

3

Getting started

This chapter outlines the practicalities and realities of setting up actual Circles of Friends around vulnerable or challenging individuals. Commitment, understanding and support will be needed from a number of key people, starting with the young person him or herself.

Taking up the challenge

The individual embarking upon the setting up of a Circle of Friends around one person is embarking on a challenging and extremely well-intentioned mission. There will be obstacles to overcome and allies to gain, but the benefits and likely outcomes will be worth the investment, however risky it may feel. The scene will need to be set, the key people briefed, the timing and place will be important. All will want to know what the point of all the effort is.

The main aims

✔ To increase the level of acceptance and inclusion of an individual.

✔ To increase the active attempts of a young person's peer group to intervene positively in that person's life.

✔ To increase opportunities for the individual to make friends in or outside the actual circle itself.

✔ To increase insight and understanding for the individual into his or her own feelings and behaviour.

✔ To provide the individual with a wider range of choices and more sense of control over his or her behaviour in a range of situations.

✔ To provide a *support team* to work actively with and relate to a vulnerable or challenging member of the school community.

Six essential steps

The first three –
1. Before you start
2. Work with the wider peer group
3. Create the Circle of Friends

The second three (see Chapter 4, p.25) –
1. The initial circle meeting
2. Hold regular meetings
3. Follow-up and review

These are described in detail in this and the next chapter.

Follow-up and review
Regular meetings
Initial meeting
Create Circle of Friends
Work with wider group
Before you start

1. Before you start

Committed staff

It is *essential* that the headteacher or senior manager and a key member of staff understand and are committed to using the approach with the young person who is the focus of concern. The key staff member, normally the class teacher or form tutor, must be able to give sufficient time to supporting the Circle of Friends in the weekly meetings that will follow the first meeting of the focus child's class or tutor group. Between 30 and 40 minutes a week will generally be needed. In some situations, this time commitment may be seen as an obstacle, but when contrasted with the time that can be spent on dealing with violent incidents, diffusing temper tantrums and the subsequent exclusion meetings, such time input begins to look minimal. The key teacher may also have to deal with issues that arise from the work for the young person, the group of pupils, for parents or even from other staff.

Committed parents

At the very start, before any work is done with the pupil's peer group, the child's parents or carers will need to have had the approach explained to them and to give both their assent and support. New issues may emerge for them, for instance when the phone rings with an invitation or children come knocking on the door requesting that their child come out to play.

Committed focus child

The focus pupil will need to have the approach properly explained in a way that he or she can make sense of with a view to the *acceptance* of what is about to occur. We have debated whether the approach could continue with less than acceptance from the individual and we are clear that it should not. When the approach is first described to a child, emotions can range from angry resistance – 'No way ...', through ambivalence – 'well maybe, but what if ...', to over-enthusiastic or unrealistic – 'I'll be cured ...!' Generally, these reactions can be worked through and it is often best to entrust this discussion to a teacher who knows the young person well.

2. Work with the wider peer group

There should be an initial meeting with the focus child's class or tutor group.

The session leader

In our work, the educational psychologist currently involved with the focus child leads this initial meeting. The meeting typically lasts for about an hour and the class teacher is present throughout and often gets involved in recording the discussion. It is important that someone with whom the class is not very familiar leads this first session. This helps reinforce the message that this is an important session and heightens the interest level. In practice, however, the headteacher, another teacher in the school or even the class teacher him or herself have successfully led these sessions.

The session aims

After introductions, the session leader should set out the aims of the meeting. These are to discuss the behaviour of the focus child and think of ways that the class can help him or her. It is worth acknowledging with the class that it is unusual to talk about someone behind his or her back, as is now being done, but that the focus child is aware of what is happening and has agreed to it.

We stress that the session is both unusual and very special. We may be talking about the named pupil this time but it could be someone else in the class on another occasion.

The person leading the meeting can then go on to say that this is a *confidential* session, private to this class. Ask for a definition of 'confidential'. Children usually understand it as meaning 'private', 'keeping what is said inside this room', 'don't blab' and so forth.

It is crucial that the class get the message at this early stage that their help is being asked for, and that the adults genuinely need their insights and ideas. Success depends on this.

A picture of the focus child

The leader should now ask the class for their picture of the focus child. Ask for the *positives* first: those things that the child does well and are enjoyed by the class and those times when things usually go well for the focus child. Everything that is said is written up for all to see. We have been continually surprised and encouraged by the ease of eliciting a detailed and positive profile of the focus child. The perceptions of the peer group are invariably more balanced and contain more positive attributions than those from the adult or staff perspective.

Your next step is to ask the class for the things *they* find *difficult* about the focus child, the things they think *he or she* finds difficult or the times when things don't go well for him or her. What is said should also be recorded alongside the earlier list of positives. Sometimes, it can be difficult to get this part of the session going fluently and the leader may need to remind the class that more honesty means a better chance of being able to help. Reluctance may be caused by feelings of loyalty to the focus child or difficulty in believing that adults really want the information that they seem to be asking for. Also, it is probably the first time that they have been asked for their views.

Who is in your relationship circles?

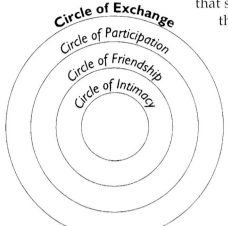

Circle of Exchange
Circle of Participation
Circle of Friendship
Circle of Intimacy

Now that the pupils' perspective on the focus child is complete, the leader of the session moves on to a more general discussion of the role of friendships. The group is encouraged to think about the differing types of relationships that surround them as individuals. We have found it helpful to structure this part of the meeting by using the picture of friendship circles.

They are told that the first circle is made up of those they are closest to and who love them. The second circle is made up of individuals that are close friends, people that they trust and may share secrets with. The third circle is peopled by a further group of friends or acquaintances, individuals that they may meet regularly at clubs, youth groups and so forth, who are part of their lives but not as close as those in the second circle. The fourth circle is made up of people with whom they have regular contacts *and* who are paid to be in their lives such as teachers, dentists, doctors, social workers and therapists.

As each circle is introduced, pupils are invited to think of people in their own lives who figure at each level and these are added to a large version of the figure for all to see.

Possible methods to use

✔ Each pupil fills in a friendship circles diagram for their own life using pictures or words.

✔ One pupil is invited to the front of the class and his or her circle is depicted on a large wall chart or on the board.

✔ Pupils are simply encouraged to imagine and think about the circles of people in their lives as they are taken through the diagram as a group.

✔ A volunteer arranges pupils around him or herself in concentric circles to represent dramatically people in his or her life.

So the group is encouraged to reflect on the richness and diversity of relationships in their own lives. The emphasis should be on the quality rather than the quantity of relationships. Care needs to be taken to ensure that individuals with few close friends are not left feeling inadequate.

The next step is a crucial one: to elicit empathic feeling in the group towards those who have very few people in their lives. The group is asked to imagine how they would feel if their second and third circles were empty and that all they had in their lives was immediate family and paid people. This is a powerful part of the session and a rich range of responses is always forthcoming. If prompts are needed, these should focus on the emptiness of Circles 2 and 3, the absence of any friends or anyone to hang around with. Here are some typical responses to the question:

How would you feel?

Lonely ... Bored ... Unhappy ... Embarrassed ... Sad ... Angry ... Like you didn't exist ... Upset ... Left out ... Invisible ... Unwanted ... As if you had no control ... Fed up with other people ... Depressed ... Like you're different ... Scared ...

The group leader then asks the class how they would act if they had these feelings. Again, a rich range of responses is readily elicited. If prompting is required, emphasis on the 'feelings' words is all that is necessary. 'How would you act if you felt lonely, left out, angry ...?'

How would you act?

Pupils know how they would behave if they had no friendships. This is the turning point in this whole-class meeting. Older classes (Year 5 (P6) and above) may have made a connection already between what they said earlier in the meeting about the focus child's behaviour and the list they have just generated. This often dramatic overlap in the two lists should be highlighted by the group leader and the class helped to think about whether some of the focus child's difficult behaviour could be a result of his or her feelings about having no friends. This can be an emotional moment for the adults present.

Ways of helping

Once the group achieves some measure of insight, the class is asked for ideas on what they could do to help the focus child. Two key tasks usually clearly emerge for the whole group:

✔ Providing the focus pupil with friendship.

✔ Developing ways of keeping the pupil on track with his or her behaviour.

Their suggestions are again listed for all to see. Typically, these suggestions from the class would be included:

> Be friendly ... Welcome him in the morning ... Invite her to play in our games ... Get him into the football team ... Tell her to stop it when she is ... Remember his birthday ... Help him with his work ... Sit next to her ... Don't call her names anymore ... Tell him it's not worth it when he loses his temper ...

This is the beginning of the problem-solving process.

A final optional brainstorming activity is designed to reinforce the openness and honesty stressed throughout. The class is asked to list what is unhelpful for the focus child. (Individuals tend to feel most comfortable with this request if allowed to report what they have seen others do rather than confessing to having done it themselves.) It has become clear to us that this public naming of what can hurt others' feelings is an important and therapeutic part of the process. Often the activities named will involve subtle ways of excluding the focus child.

3. Create the Circle of Friends

Making the selection The group leader should now enrol the supporters who will make up a Circle of Friends for the focus child. In our experience, many more children will offer than is needed to make a viable circle (six to eight members is best), so you will need a means of selecting the eventual circle. Several methods can be used to arrive at the final group. Some group leaders like to choose at random from those who have said they are willing to be involved. Others like to make their choices based on the quality of the individual's contribution to the whole-class discussion. Often it is a good idea to take the advice of the class teacher or tutor. Even better, the leader can ask the class itself who they think would be a good choice.

The focus pupil may have ideas about who would or would not be a valuable member, but their views should not dominate selection as others may be in a better place to know who needs to be part of the group. The circle may provide a setting for settling old feuds or for valuing previously disliked others. The focus pupil may be surprised and pleased by who has volunteered or may be initially antagonistic to certain children until trust in the process and clear realisation that all are there to offer support becomes a reality.

Our only advice here would be to avoid choosing only children who are perceived as well behaved by adults. These will likely be children who have had few problems of their own and experience has taught us that some of the most effective and helpful members of a Circle of Friends will be those who are seen as being quite 'difficult' themselves.

Variations on a theme

The particular process discussed above is the one we have found most effective for a focus child who is showing challenging or isolated behaviour. With a few minor alterations to what is said by the group leader, the whole-class session can also be run to enlist support for a focus child who is about to start as a new member of the class — often because he or she has been the subject of a permanent exclusion from another school. The key questions for the group would then be: 'How does it feel when you are the new person in a situation where everyone else knows each other?', 'How might you act if you felt like this?', 'What are the things that people can do that are helpful to someone who is new?' and so on.

Likewise, the session could focus on the needs of a child within the class who is experiencing learning difficulties with a view to establishing a circle of learning support. Key questions here could begin with: 'How does it feel when you don't understand what to do?' and then follow the typical sequence.

Help from all

With the Circle of Friends now chosen it is worth reminding the class as a whole that, although they might not be in the circle itself, they can still be helpful by being friendly towards the focus child, supporting the circle members and by trying to carry out the strategies they have already suggested in the brainstorming session. They also may have created a reserve list for the circle itself.

The whole process may only have taken an hour but the effects can be far-reaching. This whole-class session is central to the process and acts to sensitise the group to the needs of the focus child. Things are now out in the open and can begin to move forward. It will now be much harder for individuals to join in with teasing, excluding or victimising the focus child even if they are not part of the Circle of Friends proper.

Arrangements now need to be made for the first meeting of the circle together with the focus child. This should take place as soon after the whole-class meeting as possible.

Chapter

4

<h1>The circle in action</h1>

There are many ways of running small groups with a focus pupil at the centre. The approach we describe is only one way into this. Readers may develop their own process. Be creative but adhere to the key principles:

✔ The circle is present to support the individual's inclusion.

✔ Respect the dignity and human rights of the individual focus pupil however challenging his or her behaviour.

✔ Ensure that there is mutual support and trust.

✔ Encourage openness and honesty about feelings and behaviour.

✔ The focus pupil must feel listened to and supported, not simply challenged or threatened by the process.

1. The initial circle meeting

The initial session with the circle of volunteers sets the scene and is thus very important for all involved. The first session should be carried out as soon as is practicable after the whole-group session outlined in the last chapter. Delay will only raise concern or anxiety in the mind of the focus pupil or undue over-excitement in the potential Circle of Friends.

The first session must feel safe for the focus pupil who will experience the full *spotlight* of the peers' attention while talking frankly not only about what they like about him or her but also regarding behaviours they are unable to tolerate.

Suggested approach to running initial session

✔ Introduce self.

✔ Agree ground rules and explain confidentiality.

✔ Agree aims of group, e.g. to help focus child make and keep friends and to help him or her get back on track with his or her behaviour.

✔ Invite group members to tell child why they volunteered to be in the group.

✔ Elicit and list positives and areas the child needs to work on from the group.

✔ Brainstorm strategies.

✔ Agree which strategies can be tried and ensure commitment to these from the group. Be clear with the group about responsibilities, disclosures and boundaries. Let them know what is expected of them and the limits to this.

✔ Agree name for the group, avoiding child's name. The Tigers Group, The Helpful Group, The Listening Group and The Eclipse Group are some examples of actual choices.

✔ Describe meeting and follow-up arrangements and encourage mutual support in the group.

Introductions

The focus pupil should be well prepared for this initial circle meeting. This is best done individually before the whole-group session is run. An adult, such as the class teacher or tutor, is usually best placed to carry out this pre-session counselling. The key principle to bear in mind is that the focus pupil should not be shocked or surprised by what is being discussed with him or her. The session begins with introductions and sometimes with a warm-up activity.

Ground rules

Ground rules are introduced next. As in the whole-group session, confidentiality is both discussed and defined. It is explained that any one of the circle members could be sitting in the focus pupil's chair at some point in the future. What is being discussed is thus highly confidential to the group unless essential to the interests of the focus pupil.

Other ground rules are introduced at this stage. All rules need to be kept simple and meaningful, and might include these:

✔ Only one person speaks at a time.

✔ Act sensibly during session.

✔ Keep confidential what is spoken about during the session unless something is shared which is so important that it has to involve others.

Aim

The aims of the circle should now be clarified and restated for all present, including the focus pupil. Again the aims need to be simple and straightforward. Typically, aims might include 'getting Ruth back on track with her behaviour' and 'we are going to try to help Ruth make and keep some more friends'.

The volunteers

The next stage is often one of the most moving of the whole circle process and certainly of the initial circle meeting. Each individual circle member is asked to explain in simple terms why he or she chose to volunteer to be a member of the focus pupil's circle.

A risky start

Colin was very anxious as he sat down with his second Circle of Friends ever! He awaited in some trepidation the arrival of the focus child who was being brought to the room by his class teacher. The circle was getting restless, when outside the door could be heard a tremendous commotion. Colin felt a sinking feeling in his stomach, which was compounded when the door was thrown open and the focus pupil, Richard, was thrust inside by a red-faced teacher spluttering the words: *'He's all yours now, I'll be back at 12 o'clock!'*

Colin agonised as to whether he should call a halt immediately. He decided to continue. Richard curled up in his seat in the circle looking extremely angry and resentful. He was finding it hard even to look up or give anyone eye contact.

Having decided to proceed, the early question was posed as to why pupils had chosen to be part of his circle. By the time the fourth child had explained why he chose to volunteer to be a member of Richard's circle, he had opened up like a small but very precious flower!

The positives ...

One effective way of beginning to create an honest dialogue between the focus pupil and his or her peers is to revisit the questions posed to the whole group within this initial circle meeting. The question: 'What do we like and value about this person, what are the positives?' will usually invoke a very constructive brainstorming activity. Someone needs to write down or use graphic images on a large sheet of paper for all to see the responses to this question. The adult facilitator can make much of positive comments, can extend specific praise or even add his or her own observations.

... and the negatives

The circle needs now to examine situations where things have not gone well for the focus pupil. We have tried to avoid this becoming a long list of negatives and labels attached to the pupil concerned. Focusing on situations, rather than deficits or personality traits, seems more useful and less damaging for the individual. However, there should be no avoidance of straight, honest talk. It is crucial during this discussion to ensure that the individual continues to feel safe and not excessively threatened by this feedback as this could cause resistance. Methods of maintaining a safe climate in this situation include the following:

✔ Keep the list of difficult situations quite short.

✔ Explain in very clear terms to the focus pupil that what may be said is only what an individual feels or has experienced, it is not necessarily true, and the child should not be surprised if he or she does not agree. The circle will not be spending lots of time trying to work out what was or was not done by an individual in any given situation!

✔ Use humour to lighten up potentially difficult contributions.

✔ Challenge quickly any rule-breaking or direct attacks between members of the circle.

During this process, beware of possible sabotage from circle members bringing their own agendas into the meeting. Watch also for problematic relationships overflowing into the circle meeting itself. Old feuds, hurt feelings, resentful victims and individuals looking for revenge, all bring their own risks and tensions to the meeting. This format gives plenty of opportunities if individuals wish consciously or unconsciously to make the situation difficult for the focus pupil, and so the onus is on the facilitator to keep the meeting safe for all present.

The strategies

The next stage is to brainstorm strategies to support the focus pupil. Ideally, the focus pupil him or herself should be actively involved in contributing to this process, but it is only natural that in the initial meeting many individuals prefer to be largely silent. As above, the adult(s) present should record all ideas in words or in graphic images and, after a period of brainstorming, return to the ideas and refine them with the group. These are the key principles that underpin this process of strategy creation and acceptance:

✔ Ensure that individuals own the strategy they are suggesting. As far as possible, avoid other people being named who need to carry out the strategy, such as the class teacher.

✔ Ideas may need nurturing and developing by other group members or the adult running the group.

✔ The consequences of some ideas may need to be explored, especially if they could be counterproductive.

✔ Ensure that the focus pupil is able to accept the strategy and that he or she will cooperate with it, at least in principle, during the meeting.

✔ Commitment from circle members to strategies and ideas is essential if they are to be carried out in the real world.

A name for the group

Before closing the initial meeting, it is important to agree a name for the group. The circle should not be referred to as the *Circle of Friends* or in a way that includes the child's name. A more neutral title is preferable. Examples that have been used include the *Listening Group*, the *Reds*, the *Support Team*, the *A Team*. Circle members can generate ideas but ideally the focus pupil selects the circle name. The circle name is important for the group's identity and reinforces the mutually supporting aspects of this work.

Future arrangements

Finally, at the close of the initial meeting, follow-up arrangements need to be agreed. A meeting place, timings and availability of the adult facilitator and circle members need to be established. This meeting has been the first of a series of weekly meetings and this should be clearly stated.

Immediately after the circle breaks up, it is important to speak briefly to the focus pupil to assess the impact of this first session. If it has raised issues with the young person, a longer discussion may be required. Quite possibly, circle members will want to leave the room with the focus pupil and clearly we do not want to disrupt this unnecessarily.

2. Hold regular meetings

A weekly meeting with a key member of staff has now been set up with the six to eight volunteers. The initial meeting is usually facilitated by the group leader who has carried out the whole-group session described above, together with the teacher who is to run the group, observing and helping to record responses. The first meeting usually requires 45 minutes. Future meetings can run for approximately 20–40 minutes. Some circles have been successfully run during playtimes, assembly times or even, at a push, during registration in at least one secondary school.

A range of approaches can be used for subsequent meetings. Problem-solving processes work well and are usually relatively safe and easy to learn for all involved, and these should also allow space to explore difficult issues and celebrate successes. A main purpose of the meeting is to generate supportive ideas and practical tactics. The initial group facilitator – a visiting educational psychologist, support teacher or other – who has introduced the circle to the whole class needs to meet the class and the circle itself by the following half term or term end to follow up progress.

Possible problems

Early meetings of a Circle of Friends can be chaotic and difficult for the adult to manage constructively. Angry feelings towards the focus child are sometimes expressed or discussions are begun that have no obvious relevance to helping the child. The adult needs to remind the group of the ground rules, the reason why they are meeting and of the need to listen to each person's contribution.

For younger children (Year 3 (P4) and below), it can be helpful to structure the group meeting in ways that make the listening and turn-taking roles clearer, for instance by having warm-up and closing routines, by asking for the group's comments on set questions or by allowing group members to talk only when in possession of a special object. Objects may include a talking stick, a listening stone, a pretend microphone and so forth.

We encourage people running Circles of Friends to follow their instincts, drawing on their own gifts and experiences of talking with and working with children. Adults should have a genuine commitment to the focus pupil and be able to listen to and follow the lead of children. The focus pupil should be very carefully listened to and as far as possible increasingly allowed to guide proceedings to ensure that their needs and issues are addressed.

The need for clarity
We have found that there is a need for clear boundaries regarding how group members deal with disclosures from the focus child. The adults may wish to give clear permission for circle members to pass on any information disclosed to them that they feel they cannot keep to themselves. This may be particularly relevant to children with a history of abuse or who are believed to be at risk.

Permission and guidance is helpful with regard to what the circle members should put up with from the focus pupil. It is important to stress that they continue to have personal rights, which should not be violated. It is not acceptable for circle members to be abused physically or verbally just because they are trying to support and they need to hear this early on.

Group processes and content can vary enormously and are largely influenced by the style and strengths of the facilitator and what he or she feels able to handle or pursue. These can range from deeply emotive material to 'straightforward' behavioural strategies.

3. Follow-up and review

There is an important need for maintenance, support and follow-up sessions and for any involved outside facilitator to keep in touch, especially with a newly formed circle. Structured support, and even supervision where necessary, may be provided by some outside facilitators to those carrying out the weekly facilitation. It is well worth teachers negotiating for this, especially if new to this type of approach.

The circle facilitator
The circle leader or facilitator should contain, hold boundaries and ensure safe space for the exploration of feelings and ideas. The role is also to provide rich positives and praise and to build the esteem of the individual and the circle. The facilitator should attempt to encourage mutual support, trust, honesty and openness among the group members. This role is crucial to the success of Circles of Friends.

The commitment, skills, personal qualities and model provided by this adult deeply influence the progress of the circle in its acceptance and support of the focus pupil. In order to carry out this crucial and at times complex role, the facilitator ideally needs support and supervision in his or her work with the group from someone with appropriate psychological skills and strengths. In the busy 'real world', this may not be possible, but identifying a trusted colleague to confide in and be supported by, plus close contact with the outside facilitator if a visitor, or another member of staff with experience of group work, is essential. We all need people for support in much the same way as the focus pupil. Jack Pearpoint and Marsha Forest favour the rule of the scuba diver: *Never dive alone!*

The need for supporters

This is excellent advice for the teacher running the Circle of Friends sessions. It happens to be excellent advice to pupils within the circle also. Jack and Marsha developed this rule whilst scuba diving in Mexico. Colin learned from a British diver that diving in UK waters is particularly treacherous.

The sea is often extremely murky. In such circumstances, divers not only always dive in pairs but regularly tie their wrists together by a length of rope. Added dangers in British waters include sunken wreckage, old fishing nets and various other debris! The lesson is clear: be especially careful not to dive alone in risky situations in UK waters! (After all, who has been able to see their hands in front of their face in the murky waters of British education over the last ten years?)

Working together, circle members are also more likely to be more effective with the focus pupil. Pairs are much less vulnerable to intimidation, bullying or aggression from a highly challenging focus pupil who is being supported.

Never dive alone

One pupil, Brian, complained of being hurt quite badly when he had been alone with Scott whom he had invited to his house. He had, however, really enjoyed playing with him and had visited Scott at his home. The solution was not to stop inviting Scott but rather to include Paul, who was another circle member, in the visits.

Pupil interventions

We have been greatly impressed by the richness of the discussion and the way the group has functioned in circles, often surpassing adult problem-solving and mutual support-giving. We are also struck by the power of very simple interventions from other children. For instance:

I just say forget it ... and she does.

We just follow him out of the room and quietly ask him to come back ...

I went round to her house and asked if I could play ...

I saw him in the supermarket and I specially tried to talk to him ...

Other interventions range from the rich and varied to the mundane and adult-oriented. We are fascinated by interventions occurring outside the classroom:

We saw him getting angry with the dinner lady ... we went and started talking to him .... told him it was not worth it ... he walked away.

I told him to go back in and apologise to the teacher ...

and even outside the school:

I leant out of the window and shouted 'do you want to come swimming, Shane?' He said he couldn't, but now he comes every week with us.

Many of the pupil-generated strategies are creatively preventative:

We've invented a 'three tap code'... if he starts talking on the carpet, one of us taps the floor near him ... then he shuts up.

We are going to design a chart and write how well she has done during each lesson.

Wayne is going to sit on one side of him and I'm going to sit on the other ...

We are going to speak to Samantha because she is making her life really bad ...

Active interventions with the adult world reveal new insights into pupil perspectives on supply teachers, class teachers and midday supervisors, but are also excellent ways of calming difficult situations:

We need to invite Mr Rogers [head of year] to our next meeting to talk to him about how he is treating John.

We are going to write a letter to her mum ...

Developing circle meetings

There are a range of additional ideas and resources for those wishing to expand their repertoire of processes beyond what they can instinctively carry out or plan. Nevertheless, Circles of Friends is unlike any other group that has been set up before, so a willingness to explore and be creative, whilst respecting the pupils involved, will continue to be the most essential. One approach which lends itself well to this work is the *problem-solving approach*.

Most group problem-solving approaches follow variations on the following sequence:

✔ Review positives and negatives.

✔ Agree problem area to work on.

✔ Select and specify target.

✔ Brainstorm strategies that will help the achievement of this target.

✔ Select useful and workable strategies.

✔ Agree who will do what and when.

✔ Ensure focus pupil is comfortable, involved and accepting of agreed targets and strategies.

Another source of ideas can be drawn from Personal Development approaches.

Specific strategies for strengthening the circle and facilitating its problem-solving can be found in Bliss and Tetley, *Circle Time* (Lucky Duck Publishing, 1993), Mosley (1996) and White, Developing self-esteem in Bovair and McLaughlin (eds), *Counselling in Schools – A Reader* (David Fulton Publishers, 1993). These authors describe activities for use with children which promote the Personal Development curriculum via the use of group exercises known as 'circle time'. Amongst the key areas explored are relationships with others, issues of individual identity and responses to challenging experiences.

Useful techniques and processes may be drawn from some recent work that has focused on Social Skills developments in small groups.

Psycho- and socio-dramatic group processes lend themselves to work with Circles of Friends perhaps in relation to particular social situations that need acting out and reframing.

Therapeutic approaches towards group work derived from the humanistic, psychodynamic and counselling traditions may also be highly relevant at times. Gerda Hanko's (Hanko, 1995) work with teacher problem-solving groups is particularly relevant given the stress she places on the role of the group facilitator and the need to encourage the group to ask 'answerable questions'. Whilst these are not therapeutic groups, some of the circles seem to offer individual children opportunities to share their deepest secrets, sufferings or vulnerabilities in a healing way.

An aide-memoire for effective circle facilitation

✔ Take care that the circle does not get into the habit of racing from issue to issue as it discusses the previous week. Effective problem-solving depends on allowing time for a deeper exploration of the key areas of tension and difficulty.

✔ Learn to live with ambiguity and uncertainty over outcomes. Remember that, as the adult present, you are only likely to know the outlines of the issues, not the detail. Premature solutions, reached without a full exploration of the issues, are likely to be ineffective. Stick with 'not knowing what to do' for a bit longer.

✔ Be watchful that the focus child is not overwhelmed with questions and suggestions from the circle. The focus child is not 'on trial' and it is seldom helpful to be asked to 'explain yourself'.

✔ Leave space at the end of the session to ask if there are any worries that have not been talked through. If the 'real worries' tend to get an airing only at the very end of the session, you need to spend more time building trust within the group and encouraging them to listen supportively to each other.

✔ Remember that the circle is unlikely to arrive at a solution for everything that may be a concern. Encouraging circle members to ponder over questions between sessions can often be a helpful way of moving things on.

✔ Keep the focus on what is being achieved and how. Say what positives you have noticed and those that other staff have reported to you.

✔ And the *Golden Rule* – resist the temptation to give the circle your 'good advice'. Your role is to support them in arriving at *their* best solutions, not yours.

Graphic facilitation   There is growing interest in a method of facilitation that involves the use of a large coloured graphic to record the problem-solving process. A large sheet of paper is taped to the wall and serves as a focus for the group's discussions. The person providing the graphic facilitation makes a colourful record, using words and pictograms.

This can be a very useful aid to the running of the circle meetings and offers the following potential advantages:

✔ The richness and complexity of the whole can be seen at a glance.

✔ Links can be visually identified and connected.

✔ It is applicable to people who do not use language in typical ways.

✔ The final display becomes a group memory and can be built upon subsequently.

✔ Individual contributions are respected and valued by the act of recording. This enhances individual involvement.

✔ Latecomers to the meeting can 'catch up' quickly and those who need to leave early can revisit the discussion that they missed.

✔ Visual stimulus activates other modes of thinking.

✔ The graphic display can confirm the accuracy of what has been recorded and alter it if necessary.

✔ At a subsequent meeting, the group can quickly pick up where it left off.

✔ Colour is used to reflect and emphasise feelings.

Chapter 5

Outcomes, stories and a theory

In this chapter, we share some of our experiences of Circles of Friends in action. We explore some of the outcomes for focus pupils, other circle members, staff and ourselves. The outcomes described are diverse. This emphasises the need for staff to be open-minded about the ways the circle's work will evolve. As one headteacher said to us about his experience of running Circles of Friends, 'Things can get a bit wacky at times'.

Some case studies

Christopher's story

Christopher was a Year 6 (P7) boy attending an inner-city primary school. He had had behaviour problems since attending nursery. The same themes were present in Year 6. Christopher continued to present temper tantrums, lack of self-esteem, zero cooperation and extreme aggression, and was someone who found losing games very difficult to handle.

Staff and services involved with Christopher and his family had suspicions of physical and emotional abuse, but these were never substantiated despite numerous explorations and constant close monitoring. Christopher's parents were extremely difficult to work with. His dad was very aggressive and it was hard to get him to sit down, let alone to listen or enter into dialogue. Christopher's mum seemed anxiously protective of her son and also found it difficult to listen for that reason.

Colin had been the educational psychologist for four years and had become extremely frustrated with interventions aimed at changing Christopher's behaviour. Work with parents, behaviour programmes, target setting, reward systems and a number of other interventions had been unsuccessful. The pressure to exclude Christopher permanently grew every year. A number of teachers had found his behaviour very stressful; one had been very close to a nervous breakdown and he put this down to Christopher's presence in his class. He reported waking up in the night and picturing Christopher in front of him.

All in all, this was not a very encouraging place to start. Yet after four months of work in a Circle of Friends, Christopher had changed!

At the start of the first circle meeting, Christopher had been extremely tense and his body was wound up on his chair. However, by the time the fourth pupil had explained why he had volunteered to be part of his circle, Christopher had relaxed.

Progress is made

Within a few weeks, Christopher was no longer presenting serious tantrums. He was much better at participating in sports, more able to take the stress. He no longer talked out of turn in class. When unhappy about something, he was quicker to tell someone. Christopher had also found a new 'best mate' from a class member outside the circle.

A year later, Christopher volunteered for membership in a Circle of Friends for a pupil at his local comprehensive school. He was happy to say that he had been part of a circle in the past for himself and that this had helped him to stop hitting people and to keep him out of trouble. Two years later, Christopher continues to be successfully included in his local comprehensive school despite facing a range of challenges there. He recently recognised Colin in the school's Support Centre, saying: 'You're that man who does friends of circle, aren't you?!'

A Circle of Friends in a first grade classroom

In 'A Circle of Friends in a first grade classroom', *Educational Leadership*, 48 (3), (1990), Susan Sherwood provides an example from North America of creating a Circle of Friends for a six-year-old with severe multiple disabilities following birth trauma and head injury. Ann had moderate to severe learning difficulties, no right field vision and only a small amount of left peripheral and central vision plus a right-sided hemiplegia.

Peer support

Susan was amazed at the ability of first grade pupils to provide a structure for Ann and appropriate activities despite the absence of an adult support assistant. For example, when another pupil, Mike, noticed that Ann needed assistance, he would gather the necessary materials, quietly approach her and firmly direct the task. On one occasion when she flatly refused to participate, he unemotionally prodded her,

> 'You have to because you're a first grader, and these are the things first graders do.'

Then, without a pause, and with the same sense of purpose as an adult, he directed her to trace the letters.

Susan concludes her description of the approach with the following thoughts:

> 'As I reflect on this past year, I know that Ann's life has been touched in many ways by her peers and teachers because she was afforded a free and public education in a regular classroom. Yet the integration process isn't easy. At times, it can become all consuming. With no right answers, however, we cannot allow ourselves to be constrained by past practice. Don't be afraid to try. My vision for education is students, parents, educators, and administrators working positively to make learning positive and empowering for each student within a regular classroom.'

Simon's first circle

Simon was a Year 5 (P6) pupil in an inner-city primary school. He had been given the label of Asperger's Syndrome. Simon was experiencing great difficulties in being able to trust and respond to his peers in the ways in which they would expect him to.

Consequently, he was being 'wound up' and 'excluded' by his peers. There was considerable concern that Simon was not coping in his school. However, he was clearly stating that he wanted to stay and he was distraught when his parents decided to keep him off school. After a great deal of negotiation between Simon's parents and school staff it was agreed that Simon should have a Circle of Friends. Simon's mother and particularly his father were not sure that a Circle of Friends would be beneficial to Simon and were insistent that neither they nor Simon would want his disabilities highlighted. In their view, all Simon wanted was to be accepted as he was.

Jackie, the educational psychologist involved, arranged to initiate the Circle of Friends with Simon's class group and to facilitate the first small group meeting. During the whole-group session, Simon arrived in school with his parents and they insisted on speaking with the educational psychologist before the small group meeting took place. Jackie went to meet them amidst an air of anxiety and tension from both school staff and Simon's parents. The pupils who were to form the circle were waiting to talk with Simon in one room, together with the special needs coordinator and the special needs support assistant who were to be involved in supporting the Circle of Friends. In another room, Simon and his parents were talking with Jackie. Simon's father was angry; his son had been bullied and in his view nothing had been done. He explained that his son did not trust people easily and did not think that he was going to trust a group of six pupils. Simon's father did not want Simon to meet with the small circle.

Parental involvement

Jackie suggested that if Simon would find it difficult to meet the small group on his own, perhaps his parents could support him by being with him. Simon's parents agreed to take a big step and accompany their son into the next room to meet the support circle and staff.

Simon's peers were open and honest. Simon's parents listened. Emotions were laid bare. The young people in the room felt responsible. Simon's father felt angry but he believed the young people really did want to help his son. There was an intense feeling of caring from everyone in the room. Helping ideas flowed and Simon was clear about which ones he liked and would *accept* from the group. Simon's father spoke from the heart; he thanked the young people and shook each of their hands in turn.

Simon's circle continues to make a difference. Without the inclusion of his parents, it would not have been able to exist.

A long time coming

When the effects of what we do are far removed in time from our original actions, we typically have difficulty in seeing a connection. We are becoming increasingly aware of this failure to make links when the cause and effect have to do with our treatment of the environment, but we still need reminders that the effects of our *social* actions also may not be apparent until many years later. Consider the following research finding:

David Quinton, in 'The consequences of care: Adult outcomes from institutional rearing,' *Maladjustment and Therapeutic Education*, 5 (2), (1987), studied the adult adjustment of young women who had grown up in institutional care. He looked for factors that would help distinguish between those women who had achieved a relatively settled adult life, partly because they were able to make *planned* choices, and those whose lives were chaotic, marred by unstable and unsupportive relationships and who made few plans. A key factor that distinguished the groups was that many more of the women who had achieved some stability in their adult lives reported having had *positive experiences in school*.

Somewhere along the way the women who had done best had a teacher who had believed in them and managed to give them a sense of personal achievement. An encouraging finding, but Quinton's data enabled him to draw a further and much less obvious conclusion. He had teacher ratings of the girls' behaviour and adjustment during their school years. There was no evidence from those contemporary ratings that teachers' actions and efforts on behalf of the girls was having any effect on their behaviour *at that time*. Quinton concluded: 'People caring for such youngsters need to know that their efforts may well increase the chance of a good adult adjustment even if they do not seem to be having much immediate impact.'

Kim's circle: A headteacher's commitment was crucial

Kim, a Year 4 (P5) pupil, and her family had moved to the city to escape continual physical abuse and violence from Kim's dad towards her and her mum and brothers. Her current school and home address were her third within a year. At each new address, there had been major difficulties with neighbours, involving smashed windows, verbal abuse and intimidation.

Kim was becoming increasingly difficult to manage in her new primary school. She regularly ran out of school, sometimes going all the way home. Kim appeared isolated, caught in a bullying or victim cycle of interaction with her peers. Professionals shared concerns that Kim had been abused, although this had not been fully disclosed by either her mum or herself.

The special needs coordinator agreed that a Circle of Friends would be a useful approach for Kim. Colin was the educational psychologist and agreed to start up a circle for Kim. On the day of the whole-group session, Kim was running out of school even as Colin walked up the driveway. However, with some skilful coaxing from the staff who knew Kim well, she was persuaded to join the initial circle meeting following a very successful whole-group session.

Three meetings later, Kim's behaviour and relationships had visibly improved. The stealing and running away had apparently ceased. There had been no reports of bullying or victimisation. Colin left the first review meeting with reasons to feel extremely pleased with the early outcomes.

Perseverance is needed

One month later, on a visit to this school, Colin learned that Kim had been excluded. The Circle of Friends had abruptly ceased to run. The special needs coordinator was apologetic, but frustrated. The headteacher no longer felt able to provide cover for the class teacher who was supporting the circle on a week-by-week basis. The missing step here was that the headteacher had not been properly involved in committing to the process at the start. Inevitably, this step is crucial to the continuity of the work. Negotiations began again to get the circle up and running once more. The story continues …

Nicky's circle:
A circle of
learning support

Nicky was a Year 5 (P6) pupil who had difficulties in using and understanding spoken language in the usual ways. As a result, he was often unsure what was expected of him in class and frequently the work he produced was below a level expected for someone of his age. Nicky excelled at sport and PE and gained the respect of his peers because of this. Staff felt Nicky was well liked by his classmates. He had received two hours' support each day from a classroom assistant for a number of years and it was Nicky's response to this support that was causing concern. Nicky had become increasingly reluctant to accept support and unwilling to attempt new learning tasks. He seemed to be losing all confidence in himself and in his ability as a learner. The only time he seemed happy was playing football in the playground.

Derek, the educational psychologist for Nicky's school, discussed with staff the idea of using a Circles of Friends approach to try to improve things. It was not immediately obvious how a circle could be helpful. After all, Nicky did not lack friendships and was popular. However, we felt that anything that could reduce Nicky's feelings of isolation in class might be helpful.

A variation

Some changes were needed to the key 'How would you feel? How would you act?' questions used in the initial whole-class session. We asked them to tell us how they felt and acted when they did not understand what they were supposed to be doing with a piece of classwork. These questions exposed a rich vein of pupil experience. Everyone readily identified with the 'when you don't know what to do' scenario. They knew the negative feelings this provoked and could tell us about the strategies they employed to deal with the situation, including going to the toilet for long periods, endlessly sharpening pencils, disappearing into the book corner and hoping not to be noticed, copying from neighbours and so on. It was a short step from this to identifying the things that others can do that are helpful to the person in this situation and this brainstorming gave us many ideas that were later shared with Nicky in the small group meeting.

Many of the things the circle members did for and with Nicky were low key and simple, just small acts of reassurance and confirmation in the course of a lesson. However, this circle got to the heart of the matter when they suggested that Nicky's support assistant should spend more time working with him in a small group rather than being with him by herself. Children know what makes them feel included and this circle was successful in doing this for Nicky. His attitude to work and his acceptance of support improved greatly as a result.

Arundeep's circle: A snapshot of pupil perceptions

Arundeep was a Year 3 (P4) pupil who had nearly been permanently excluded for aggression towards other pupils and staff in his inner-city primary school. Problems at home had fuelled an explosive temper and he had become isolated, friendless, disruptive in class and uncooperative. The following quotations indicate how a Circle of Friends helped Arundeep.

Facilitator: What's changed since the group started at the beginning of term?

Circle members: Lots of things.

Facilitator: What are the positives?

Circle members: He doesn't lose his temper now.
We trust him now.
He is picking his friends more wisely now.
His friends are closer now.
He does not answer back so much.
He has learned to say sorry.
He is closer to Jay [another pupil] now.

Facilitator: What things are still issues you are working on?

Circle members: He still needs to work on finishing his writing off.
He got sent in the hall for jumping on someone's back.

Facilitator: What things have you done to support him?

Circle members: We have created a chart for him. Five signatures mean he can sit on a chair at carpet time!
We give him more chances.
We have helped him to keep calm.
We have helped him with targets. For instance, if he doesn't shout, we reward him.
We have supported him so that he walks away from arguments with staff.
We try to prevent arguments.
We have talked him out of temper tantrums.
We have lent pencils to him to prevent arguments.

Some final thoughts

Sometimes staff will judge that a whole-class session is not an appropriate starting point. This will usually be the case when the intended focus child already has a group of friends in Circle Two and the aim is to mobilise them to support him or her through a particular crisis, for example a serious illness or a significant bereavement.

In these kinds of situations, the facilitator can discuss with the focus pupil whom he or she would like to invite to be part of the circle of support and then make direct requests for help to those named. It can be useful as part of this process to ask the focus child to fill in the relationships diagram reproduced on p.62. This will help to clarify who is in this person's life and may be an important circle member.

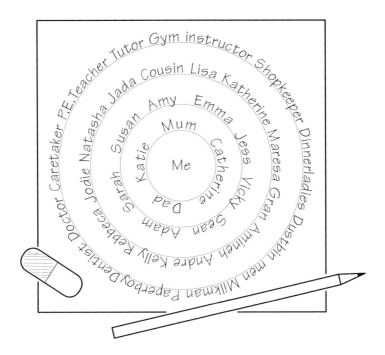

Membership need not be confined to other pupils attending the same school. Indeed, anyone who has a close relationship and is willing to become involved is a potential circle member. Again, our advice is to be creative. Increasingly, we are trying to widen and strengthen circle membership and have successfully included people who do not usually figure in our planning meetings, such as the focus person's sister's boyfriend, the school caretaker, or a grandparent.

The message is that diverse voices provide diverse solutions to the difficulties being faced.

Is there a theory to go with it?

This is primarily a workbook and values primer. It does not aim to explore the various theoretical constructs that can be used to go deeper into the psychological and social processes behind Circles of Friends work. None the less, it is worth looking at the further insights that are gained when circles work is viewed from a particular theoretical standpoint – *Social constructionism*.

Social constructionism is the name given to a relatively recent philosophical approach to the social sciences. The core construct of social constructionism is that the way we understand the world and ourselves is the result of the processes of interaction between groups of people. From this perspective, ideas only have meaning inasmuch as they are shared and agreed by others and the belief that there are universal truths which can be discovered by science and hold true for all time is rejected. Instead, what is seen to be true in a given place and time is a product of the social and historical context within which the ideas were developed and negotiated.

The key process by which ideas are given meaning by human societies is *narrative* – the stories we tell to make meanings. These stories are not viewed as simply the product of individual minds but are seen as being *created* in the shared space between the narrator and the audience. Thus there is a sense in which we do not know what we think until we attempt to relate this to others. Likewise, we gain our sense of what is *possible* (what can be constructed with others) through the act of narrating. If we take a social constructionist position, then by sharing stories we learn more about who we are and who we might become.

Circles of Friends provide a setting in which a social world can be created and, as a result, deeper understandings of one another are found.

'The problem' should not be seen as a deficit of some sort within the focus person, but should be viewed instead as a narrative that has grown up between the focus person and the key players in that person's life – classmates, teachers, family members and so on. The problem is something that all involved act out and the role of the focus person is to play his or her part in the story.

The 'dominant narrative' in the lives of people with disabilities will typically contain themes that emphasise dependency, developmental limitation, inability to contribute to society, lack of relationships or participation and a host of similarly constraining 'stories'. However, if we view these stories as socially mediated constructs rather than as evidence of underlying and immutable deficits, then it follows that action can be taken to rewrite the narrative and repair the stories in a way that is less costly to the focus person. This is possible because no *one* story ever encompasses all the feelings and experiences of the focus person. Less noticed parts of their interactions can be brought to the fore and woven into a fresh narrative.

From theory to practice

We would argue that this way of construing social action and what is therapeutic fits well with our experience of Circles of Friends in action. When a Circle of Friends is formed, the focus child is given a forum within which he or she can be supported in re-authoring the dominant narrative of his or her life. Members of the circle support this by contributing their knowledge of the 'less noticed' focus child and by acting in ways that help to bring these new parts of the narrative to life. Thus new aspects of the child are appreciated which no one had even noticed previously.

Notice also that, from this perspective, the story never ends, no one is 'cured' and life goes on in a more or less happy way depending on how well a new narrative can be created. As Jack Pearpoint often says, 'Inclusion is simple ... but it is not easy, we are given a lifetime to figure it out.'

'Stories' and the reconstruction of disability

A growing number of independent and self-supporting groups are forming in the UK and elsewhere to campaign for equality of opportunity for children and adults labelled disabled. One such group is the Sheffield-based 'Parents With Attitude' and readers are encouraged to get hold of their book *Let Our Children Be*. This book is subtitled *A collection of stories* and it is a deliberate attempt to reframe the lives and relationships of children with disabilities by publishing the narratives that are rarely heard – those of parents, siblings and friends of the disabled child.

Several of these narratives are hostile to the dominant (medical) narrative of disability with its emphasis on deficit and treatment. Many of the writers take care to emphasise how their lives and learning have been enriched by their experiences of being a parent of a child with a disability. This is in direct contradiction to the dominant narrative which only has stories of the 'burdens' carried by parents, their need for respite, the risk of marital breakdown and so on.

One of the aims of *Let Our Children Be* is to bring into being an alternative narrative of disability and, by so doing, let others know that they are not alone in what they might be thinking and to give them permission to see the world in other ways. In such ways is social reality constructed and in the field of disability there is a rich fund of powerful and life-enhancing stories waiting to be told.

> Why would you change him?
> Don't you realise that I can feel
> Your need to change him
> Your need for him to be other than as he is
> To be improved
> To be more or less or whatever
> You are disturbed by?
> Don't you understand that
> The comments you make about my child
> Tell about yourself
> And not about him?
> And the needs we discuss
> Are yours
> And not his
> When you look at my child

Jill Penman, *Let Our Children Be*

Chapter

6

Questions

Twelve frequently asked questions

In the past four years, we have made many in-service training presentations on inclusion and Circles of Friends. On most occasions, our audience has been practising teachers, educational psychologists or members of other LEA support services. This section contains a selection of the most common questions we have been asked and our evolving answers to them.

A note of caution is needed. The answers are our answers, not *the* answers or even your answers. We cannot know what will work best in your context, we can only say what has seemed to work in similar settings. It is for this reason that we urge you to be creative in how you apply the ideas in this book to the situation you are working in. As long as you have one eye fixed on the deeper values and principles behind Circles of Friends, you are free to find your own ways to build relationships and community in your workplace or family.

Question 1

What if, at the end of the whole-class session, no one shows a willingness to be part of the focus child's circle?

This is probably the most frequently voiced anxiety from anyone contemplating running the circles process. It is still experienced by those who have already run several successful sessions with different classes and tutor groups. Often this fear is fuelled by other adults around the child who may have experienced considerable frustration when trying to change the child's behaviour or when they have had to placate other pupils who have been made angry or fearful by the focus child. Our and many others' experience is that this fear is never realised if the facilitator has recruited the right people and asked the key questions from the heart, that is, as if they mattered.

Sometimes the whole-class session will be used by individual pupils as an opportunity to express their anger and frustration with the focus child. As long as the facilitator provides a boundary for these strong feelings and does not allow the session to become solely about complaining, it is helpful for this to happen – the message is that this is real and people are being listened to. With these feelings off their chests, the class is more likely to be able to move on and look at ways forward to help the focus child.

If, at the stage of enlisting support, things seem to be sluggish or uncertain, it is often helpful to put the recruitment issue back to the class by asking, 'Is there anyone who people think would be a helpful member of the circle and who hasn't yet come forward?' Groups always have suggestions when asked this and they are usually the right ones. The individuals nominated in this way usually agree!

Question 2

What would you do with a child that smells? Surely you couldn't build a circle for them?

The answer is: 'Build a Circle of Friends!' Friends are people who care enough to notice and tell the truth.

We like to put the answering of this question back to the person who asked it. Often hard questions like this are easier to think about and imagine solutions to if you personalise them. Therefore ask yourself: 'Who would tell you if you smelled?', 'Who would you be angry with for not telling you?', 'Who could you bear to hear this news from?'. These are answerable questions in a way that the anonymous 'What would you do with a child that smells?' is not. Put in a personal way, it is easier to think what you might do and therefore to have ideas for what could be done for the focus child. Another approach to answering this question is to remember that the person who smells may be aware of this but does not have a means of asking for help to overcome the problem. A Circle of Friends provides a context in which help can be sought.

Question 3

I can think of at least seven children in my class who would benefit from this approach. Should I run circles for each of them?

We doubt whether this would be manageable using the process we describe and likewise, we would not recommend that a circle has more than one focus child within it. However, we would recommend that readers get hold of a very useful paper by John Luckner, a professor of special education at the University of Northern Colorado (Luckner *et al.*, 1994). Here they will find a description of a personal and social education programme that was focused on a group of eight Year 5 and 6 pupils, all of whom were described as having difficulty in making and keeping friends.

This peer network included a child with a significant hearing loss about whom there were particular concerns regarding his lack of relationships within the class and the impact of his hearing loss on his chances of forming closer friendships. However, he was not the focus of the group's concerns. Each pupil in the group was asked to commit to attend the 'friendship sessions' for at least eight weeks. Luckner's paper describes the sequence of relationship-building activities that the group followed in their weekly meetings. The informal evaluations carried out at the end of the programme make it clear that there are many positive gains to be had from this low-key approach to relationship building. This piece of work also underlines the point that making and sustaining relationships is an area of tension for all pupils, not simply those labelled different or disabled.

Question 4

What if a disclosure is made during the circle meeting?

It is important, when briefing a new Circle of Friends, to ensure that all realise that they may be told something which they cannot keep secret or confidential. Pupils will need to be reminded that if they hear something important or worrying about or from the focus child, they should speak to an adult such as the teacher running the circle. It is quite possible that a disclosure could be made to an individual or within the group meeting itself. One of the strengths of the approach is that pupils learn to trust one another. Secrets and private sufferings have, in our and others' experience, been safely shared in the most successful circles.

Question 5

What about circle members who become 'over-enthusiastic'?

Some circle members quickly become very enthusiastic to support, befriend and bring about change in the focus pupil. Such enthusiasm may be very endearing to the facilitator or teacher attempting to set up a new circle, but clearly there are pitfalls to such enthusiasm. Disappointment, over-zealous watchfulness or leaving themselves vulnerable to bullying or violent outbursts or just being unable to cope with the focus child's needs are among some of these. Careful support, encouragement and guidance may be needed from the adult running the circle or indeed further frank and honest discussion between circle members about the issue may be helpful. The key message to the individual circle members is: *Never dive alone!*

Individuals within the circle should always be encouraged to work together and to avoid situations in which they may become vulnerable. Escorting a pupil home, visiting a pupil in his or her home, playing in an isolated area and so forth can be potentially dangerous for an individual pupil and they are much safer when there is more than one circle member involved in whatever activity is planned.

Question 6

Can circles co-opt members?

Yes. Stronger, older peers, relations, or even adults may at times be usefully co-opted into the circle and strengthen its work. Diversity brings strength and this is at the root of circle work. The right people who can make a difference to the individual need to be present. Sometimes the right person to co-opt is the one who is giving the circle most concerns because of his or her antagonism towards the focus child. A constructive way of viewing this antagonism is to say that this child also has an unmet need to belong. Inviting him or her to be part of the circle is a step towards meeting this need and will likely deal with the antagonism at the same time.

Question 7   *What other ways are there to encourage friendship?*

Just being with other children can be a critical variable in the development of friendships for the most vulnerable, especially those being educated in segregated settings. Mainstream classroom techniques to encourage friendships can include mentoring systems, peer tutoring, buddy schemes and cooperative learning groups (Luckner and McDonald, Teaming to Learn, *Perspectives on Deafness*, 10 (1), (1992)). Schools can encourage disabled and able-bodied pupils to get involved with other children in such extra-curricular activities as chess clubs, team sports, photography, and any variety of outdoor activities. Assemblies and lessons that focus on the importance of friendship and supportive relationships can helpfully be built in throughout the school curriculum.

Reading and discussing books about friendship, such as *Friends* by H. Heine, (MacMillan, 1985), is another straightforward way to promote the learning of friendship skills. Enrolling or inducting new pupils provides an excellent opportunity for teaching these skills. Discussion about pupils can focus on ways to help the newcomer feel welcome and secure. A welcoming committee can be formed or one or more class members can be assigned as *buddies* to help the new pupil adapt to classroom routines, the daily timetable and the physical geography of the school. Teachers should always be alert for opportunities to suggest meaningful interactions among pupils, building on their observations of children working together.

Teachers can arrange for pupils who need friends to work with more sociable classmates on activities such as cleaning blackboards, watering plants, carrying materials from car to school, or from room to room, running errands or returning books to the library. Within all of this, what are the key peer support skills we should focus on?

Luckner *et al.* (1994) provide an excellent response to this question as follows:

✔ Developing positive interactions: the skills of being positive, attentive, approving, encouraging and interested.

✔ Finding areas of compatibility: shared interests are the most common basis for friendship. Pupils need to understand the importance of expressing interest in the concerns and experiences of others, as well as their own.

✔ Empathising with others: learning to be understanding and sensitive to the concerns and feeling of others.

✔ Sharing and providing support: pupils need to learn to help, support and share with others, especially in times of need.

✔ Building trustworthiness and loyalty: pupils need to understand the concepts of honesty and loyalty as well as the specific behaviours that these require.

✔ Developing skills for conflict resolution: learning to protect one's own interests assertively without being either submissive or aggressive is a major challenge for both pupils and many adults.

Question 8

What is the best way to choose circle members?

This question is covered in Chapter 4. There are many ways in which a circle can be formed including the following:

✔ Random selection of pupils: Any random technique such as picking names from a hat can be used.

✔ Teacher selection: Teachers may wish to make their own selection of ideal circle members for the focus pupil. (We do not encourage this option as it can run the risk of old cycles of preference and selection taking precedence over other more important factors.)

✔ Facilitator selection: The facilitator makes the choice on the basis of contributions to the whole-class session. (We do not prefer this method as a silent member of the whole-group session may hold an essential key to relationships with the focus pupil.)

✔ Pupil selection: The class or tutor group simply nominate a number of pupils who they feel to be best suited to support the focus pupil. They can be prompted to consider shared interests, hobbies or other activities or to consider other strengths of fellow classmates including strong personality, communication skills, negotiation skills, popularity and, most importantly, street credibility.

✔ A compromise involving facilitator, teacher and pupil selection: The facilitator and the teacher each choose two members on the basis of their knowledge of the class or tutor group and the pupils choose the rest. At the time of writing, this is the method of selection we are using most often. But remember – what works best for us may not be best for you.

✔ The focus pupil selects members of his or her circle from volunteers: The focus pupil is given the names of volunteers and is asked to suggest other names of pupils who would be most helpful, supportive and usefully challenging within his or her Circle of Friends. This would provide maximum control to the focus pupil and strengthen his or her ownership but would also contain some disadvantages. There is a security and a sense of clear boundaries for a focus pupil who is able to meet an already formed circle where all have volunteered and have been selected using methods drawn from the above list.

Question 9   *How long do children need to remain as members of the circle?*

We have already stressed the need for the facilitator to provide boundaries for the circle members in order to allow safe expression of feelings. Time boundaries are also important and it can be helpful to let prospective circle members know that their commitment will be expected for a set period (a school term is a useful block of time) and that after this, they will have the choice of continuing for a further period or of opting out for a spell. In practice, we have found that opting out is rare in successful circles: however, circle members find it reassuring to know that they can.

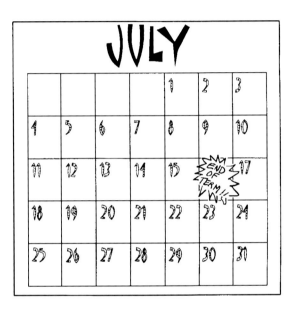

Question 10   *Can the circle meet without the focus child present?*

Strictly speaking, this is not an option that has any place in an authentic approach to Circles of Friends work. The circle is built around the focus child who must have the final say on decisions taken and the power to influence how things are viewed by others. This is unlikely to be possible if he or she is not at the meeting.

In practice, much will depend on the skills of the facilitator and his or her ability to enable difficult issues and individual circle members' frustrations to be aired in a constructive way. Some facilitators have felt the need to convene a circle meeting without the focus child present. This has usually occurred when things appear to be going badly, and the efforts of circle members are felt to be having little effect on identified issues and it is felt that they would benefit from a chance to offload some of their frustrations. This may be a helpful step to take if the alternative is the collapse of the circle, but if you are finding that you are having frequent circle meetings without the focus child, you have strayed way off track and are no longer facilitating a Circle of Friends.

Question 11

What if it all goes wrong?

This work does involve risks. Human relationships involve risks. But the risks of doing nothing or of staying with tried and tested methods are much greater. Remember, Circles of Friends can actually stop children being excluded or segregated. Particular risks in school settings that are worth being aware of, when using Circles of Friends, include the following:

✔ *Sabotage.* This may be caused by senior members of staff or by colleagues and has a variety of motivations. Sabotage can occur in all innocence as a result of chaotic planning, or can arise from a lack of understanding of the Circles of Friends process.

✔ *Continuity breaks.* Things can get off track when circle meetings are brought to an untimely end due to cover problems, staff absence or the work not being seen as high priority. This breaks the flow and commitment of the circle and is particularly unhelpful to the focus pupil.

✔ *Feelings of exclusion.* Other members of staff may be unwittingly threatened by the relationship you have formed with the focus child and his or her circle. They may feel deskilled by the enthusiasm you have created or resentful of the time you have found or negotiated for your work with the circle. Whatever triggers these feelings, the associated behaviours can be potentially destructive. Beware.

✔ *Over-enthusiasm.* This can lead to individual circle members placing themselves in high-risk situations with the focus pupil. Individuals always need reminding to work together in mutual support rather than going it alone.

✔ *Parental anxiety.* Parents of the focus pupil or parents of members of the circle may become unduly anxious about the Circles of Friends work. This usually occurs where parents have not been properly informed about what is happening or are relying on rumour, or reacting to a particular event.

At other times, if you are not confident or comfortable with the direction in which things are going, you will have the option of having further consultations with whoever provided the initial external facilitation. When things get difficult, it is often because the circle has been over-ambitious in its early planning and its expectations of being able to make a difference. Try to simplify and reduce the number of aims being worked towards. Assess the risks within your own situation and plan your action accordingly. This work is worth the risk! You should always aim to work together with another person, possibly a colleague, and always ensure that individuals in the key positions within your school setting fully understand and support what you are trying to do.

Never go it alone!

Question 12   *What if ... ?*

This is the last question, and it is not really a frequently *asked* question but it may be a frequently *thought* question. If there is an answer, it is that sometimes we have *no idea* what the way forward is. This answer is a counsel against the culture of professionalism that implies that every situation is covered and every question has an answer if only we knew who we should refer to. To be able to say with honesty that you don't know what to do next is often a therapeutic thing to do. It passes the power back to the person that is seeking help.

APPENDIX A: USEFUL HANDOUTS

TRACKING DOCUMENT

Circles of Friends for:

Date:

Name of circle:

Pupils present:

Meeting place: Review date:

Positives	**Issues**

Discussion points:

Agreed action:

Signed:

REVIEW

Circles of Friends for:

Facilitated by:

Outside facilitator:

Date:

Name of circle: Circle started on:

Meeting place: Who was present at review?

Names of pupils involved in circle:

Were any circle meetings cancelled?   Reason:

Attendance at meetings?

    Full   Partial

Behaviour changes reported by:

Staff	Parents	Pupils	Circle pupils

Positives of approach: **Emerging issues:**

Future action:

AN INTRODUCTION TO CIRCLES OF FRIENDS

A staff guide

These brief notes will give you some background information and an idea of what would be entailed in setting up and running a Circle of Friends in your school.

1. Circles of Friends originated in North America as one of a range of strategies to encourage the inclusion of children with disabilities into mainstream settings. Circles have been used to support children with a wide range of disabilities and have also been used in the community. The approach has been developed in Nottingham, Bristol and elsewhere in the UK and has been shown to be very effective.

2. A circle usually consists of 6–8 volunteers (most often from the same class or tutor group) who meet regularly (usually weekly) with the 'focus child' and an adult. The circle has three main tasks: to offer encouragement and recognition for successes and progress; to identify difficulties, set targets and devise strategies for achieving targets; and to help to put these ideas into practice.

3. Setting up a circle includes the following steps:

    ✔ Gaining the support and agreement of the focus child and his or her parents.

    ✔ A meeting with the whole class (which the focus child does not attend) aimed at identifying those willing to be supporters, which takes roughly 30–40 minutes.

    ✔ Informing the parents of those chosen to be circle members and gaining their agreement to their children's participation.

    ✔ Weekly meetings of the circle, the focus child, and an adult facilitator (taking 20–30 minutes).

AN INTRODUCTION TO CIRCLES OF FRIENDS

A parents' guide

1. What is a Circle of Friends?

A circle is a group of 6–8 youngsters who have volunteered to meet regularly with your child and a teacher (usually this is for 20–30 minutes per week).

2. What is a Circle for and what happens?

The circle has four main aims:

✔ To create a support network of other pupils for your child.
✔ To help your child cope more easily in school and give him or her more choices.
✔ To provide your child with encouragement and recognition for any achievements and progress.
✔ To work with your child in identifying difficulties and coming up with practical ideas to help to sort these out.

The adult is there to help the circle, but the youngsters do the work with your child – coming up with ideas, trying things out, reporting back.

The circle can't provide instant friendship – but we hope that it will help your child to build closer and better connections and relationships with other children.

3. How will it be set up?

The members of your child's class would be asked if they are interested in being part of the circle. Your child's teacher will explain to them what this involves – usually this is best done when your child is not actually in the room.

We almost always end up with more pupils who are willing to help than we need and your child's class teacher will be involved in selection along with other class members. The group then meets regularly with an adult.

4. Will it help?

Obviously we can't guarantee this. However, Circles of Friends has been used quite widely in Canada, America and increasingly in this country. Evaluations in this country have so far been very positive and have helped children who have had complex difficulties and disabilities:

✔ Children at the centre of the circles have often shown improved behaviour and less worry about mixing with their classmates.
✔ The volunteers have been very good at coming up with creative and practical ideas.
✔ Most volunteers have been keen to continue their involvement.
✔ School staff have found the circles to be very worthwhile.

Please contact . . . . if you would like to discuss 'Circles' in more detail or if you have any questions or concerns.

A LETTER TO PARENTS OF VOLUNTEERS

Dear

The school has become involved in a project to set up and run what are called Circles of Friends. These are made up of 6 to 8 children who have agreed to help one of their classmates. Usually the Circles help someone to get on with other children. It involves the group in meeting once a week for 20–30 minutes (during lunchtime) with a teacher and the focus child to come up with solutions and ideas for sorting out any difficulties.

The idea is being used in other parts of the country. As well as helping the focus child, it has been found to have benefits for all the young people in the Circle. In particular, it seems to help them to develop their ability to think through problems and helps with their understanding of themselves and others.

<Child's name> has agreed to be part of the Circle (though of course may opt out after an agreed time). We are very grateful for <child's name>'s willingness to become involved and we hope that you are happy with this. If you have any concerns or questions, please let us know as soon as possible.

THE WHOLE-CLASS MEETING – RECRUITING VOLUNTEERS

1. **Introduction**
    a) Explain your involvement with focus child.
    b) Explain your interest in how youngsters get on with and can help each other.

2. **Ground rules**
    a) Treat each other with respect.
    b) Listen … one person speaking at a time.
    c) Confidentiality.

3. **Need to talk about focus pupil**
    a) Emphasise this is unusual (to talk behind someone's back).
    b) Focus pupil knows this is happening.
    c) Reason is that you need their help to think about ways in which focus pupil can be helped (stress need for/ value of their insights).

4. **Need for confidentiality (explain)**
    a) No reference to who said what about whom – the details stay in this class.
    b) Emphasise that this confidentiality also binds adults.

5. **Listing positives**
    a) Focus on positives first – good at …, nice things about …, what the focus child does well.
    b) List all contributions on a flip chart.

6. **Where things do not go so well/ difficult times for focus child**
    a) Explain that you've heard about some difficulties, but probably not all.
    b) Ask for descriptions of behaviour – list.
    c) Describe sort of person he or she is – list.

7. **Discussion of friendships**
    a) Display circle diagram (p.62) and introduce the circles:
        i)   People you love and who love you   iii) Friends/acquaintances
        ii)   Allies/best friends   iv)   People paid to be in your life.
    b) Fill in a volunteer's circles on the flip chart with help from class.
    c) All fill in own circle diagram privately.

8. **What would it be like if …**
    a) What would it be like if Circles 2 and 3 had no people in them?
    b) How would it feel? – make a list.
    c) How would they behave? – make a list. Compare to flip chart from 6.

9. **List ideas to support focus child: enlist empathy, support and commitment**

10. **What's involved**
    a) Explain about the idea of Circles of Friends and that you want to set up a group which will help with <child's name>'s difficulties.
    b) Explain what would be required, e.g. meeting at lunchtime once a week.
    c) Explain that only six to eight will be involved.
    d) Pass out small pieces of paper. Ask them to think about whether they would like to volunteer, then to write their name on the paper with *either* a yes or a no. Stress confidentiality and 'no pressure'.
    e) Explain that not everyone will be able to do it *but*
        i)   may need new people in group at later date.
        ii)   everyone can take responsibility for helping.
        iii) letter home to all parents of those chosen, explaining about it.

THE FIRST MEETING OF THE CIRCLE

1. Introductions.

2. Restate ground rules.

   a) Listen to each other.
   b) Treat each other as we would like to be treated.

3. Reminder of the aims.

   a) To work with <child's name> to help him or her make friends.
   b) To help him or her identify and sort out difficulties.
   c) To support each other in helping <child's name>.

4. Ask each to state reason for wanting to be in group.

5. Ask group to list positives (point out that <child's name> didn't hear what was said at first session). Ask <child's name> to add any to list.

6. Ask group to list situations where things do not go so well and what <child's name> needs to work on.

   a) Ask for descriptions of behaviours.
   b) Turn each problem behaviour into a positive target (describing what <child's name> should be doing rather than *not* doing).
   c) Ask <child's name> to add to any of lists a) or b).
   d) Talk about what would be different if <child's name> achieved these targets – for him or her and for others.

7. Introduce problem-solving.

   a) Explain need to work on one or two targets at a time.
   b) Ask group to decide which target(s) (including <child's name> in discussion). Suggest that it may be best to start with something quickly achievable.
   c) Brainstorm possible ways to get to the target.
   d) Select jointly and help group spell out steps.
   e) Agree responsibilities and boundaries (emphasise that <child's name> is responsible for own behaviour).
   f) Emphasise realism about speed of change, setbacks, etc.

8. Agree name for group.

9. Arrange next meeting.

SUBSEQUENT MEETINGS OF THE CIRCLE

1. **Warm-up/settling-in exercise**

2. **Good news**

    a) Ask for any situation involving <child's name> which went well (involving or witnessed by the members)

         i) Get detail as to what <child's name> said or did.

         ii) Explore how participants felt.

    b) Ask for any success in working towards targets.

3. **Bad news**

    a) Discuss any blockages in steps towards target.

    b) Brainstorm solutions.

    c) Any other problems.

4. **Target setting**

    a) Maybe more of same, different means to same end, or a new target.

    b) Brainstorm solutions (if not already done in 3b).

    c) Plan detail and agree responsibility and action.

RELATIONSHIPS DIAGRAM
Concentric circles

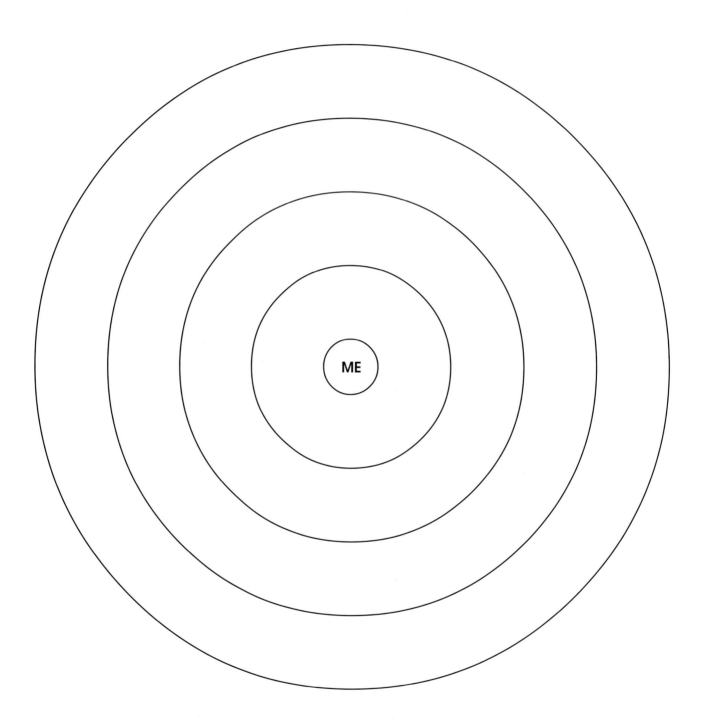

APPENDIX B: RESOURCES

This section contains references, organisations and resources relating to the vision and practice of inclusion and, in particular, to work with Circles of Friends or support. Some of the materials referenced can only be obtained in the UK through Inclusion Distribution, the UK outlet for Inclusion Press. We have also included some websites that we think are worth a visit.

References

Falvey, M. A., Forest, M., Pearpoint, J. and Rosenberg, R., *All My Life's a Circle – Using the Tools: Circles, Maps and Path* (Inclusion Press, 1994)

Gray, C. A. and Garand, J. D., Social stories: Improving responses of students with autism with accurate social information, *Focus on Autistic Behaviour*, 8 (1), (1993)

Hanko, G., *Special Needs in Ordinary Classrooms – From Staff Support to Staff Development*, 3rd ed. (David Fulton Publishers, 1995)

Jordan, L. and Goodey, C., *Human Rights and School Change – The Newham Story* (The Centre for Studies in Inclusive Education, Bristol, 1996)

Lovett, H., *Learning to Listen: Positive Approaches and People with Difficult Behaviour* (Jessica Kingsley, 1996)

Luckner, J., Schauermann, D., and Allen, R., Learning to be a friend, *Perpectives on Deafness*, 12 (5), (1994)

McLeod, J., *Narrative and Psychotherapy* (Sage Publications, 1997)

Mosley, J., *Quality Circle Time in the Primary Classroom* (LDA, 1996)

Murray, P. and Penman, J., *Let Our Children Be. A Collection of Stories* (Parents with Attitude, c/o 44 Cowlishaw Road, Sheffield S11 8XF, 1996)

Newton, C. and Tarrant, T., *Managing Change in Schools* (Routledge, 1992)

Pearpoint, J., Forest, M. and Snow, J., *The Inclusion Papers – Strategies to Make Inclusion Work* (Inclusion Press, 1993)

Perske, R. and Perske, M., *Circles of Friends* (Abingdon Press, 1988)

Shaw, L., *Each Belongs – Integrated Education in Canada* (The Centre for Studies in Inclusive Education, Bristol, 1990)

Snow, J., *What's Really Worth Doing and How to Do it* (Inclusion Press, 1994)

Thomas, G., Inclusive schools for an inclusive society, *British Journal of Special Education*, 24 (3), (1997)

Villa, R. A. and Thousand, J. S., *Creating an Inclusive School* (Paul H. Brookes Publishing, 1995)

Wertheimer, A., *Circles of Support – Building Inclusive Communities* (Circles Network, Bristol, 1995)

Whitaker, P., Barratt, P., Joy, H., Potter, M. and Thomas, G., Children with autism and peer group support: Using circles of friends, *British Journal of Special Education* (1998)

Books and videos published or produced by Inclusion Press are available in the UK from Inclusion Distribution, 29 Heron Drive, Poynton, Stockport SK12 1QR
Tel: 01625 859146

The Alliance for Inclusive Education can be contacted at Unit 2, 70 South Lambeth Road, London SW8 1RL   Tel: 0171 735 5277

Circles Network can be contacted through Mandy Neville, Director, Circles Network, Pamwell House, 160 Pennywell Road, Upper Easton, Bristol BS5 0TX
Tel: 0117 939 3917

Video material

With a Little Help from my Friends available from Inclusion Distribution.

Altogether Better by Richard Rieser and Micheline Mason available from Comic Relief Education, Unit 2, Drywall Estate, Castle Road, Sittingbourne, Kent ME10 3RL.

Kids Belong Together available from Inclusion Distribution.

Circles of Support – the companion video to the book *Circles of Support – Building Inclusive Communities* available from Circles Network.

NEW MAPS Training Video Shafik's Map (plus ... *'Dreaming'* with **Judith Snow**) available from Inclusion Distribution.

Websites on the Internet

http://inclusion.com
Links to other websites dealing with inclusion and lists resources produced by Inclusion Press.

http://www.lsi.ukans.edu/beach/beachhp.htm
Training and dissemination activities to aid inclusion of children with disabilities.

http://www.asri.edu/CFSP
Assistance to those developing inclusive educational and community supports.

http://www.grove.com/
The leading authority on graphic facilitation and other process tools.

http://funrsc.fairfield.edu/~jfleitas/contkids.html
Issues relating to children with chronic medical conditions at school.

http://www.downsyndrome.com
Practical approaches to inclusion of pupils with disabilities in mainstream schools.

http://www.mailbase.ac.uk/lists-p-t/senco-forum/welcome.html
Active debates on current special needs issues.

http://www.innotts.co.uk/~colinn/epsweb.htm
The authors' website. Links to a number of the above sites and others of interest.

http://www.oise.on.ca/~bwillard/facinfo.htm
Ideas and links relevant to facilitation skills and process tools.

http://soeweb.syr.edu/thechp/hppress.htm
A policy, research and advocacy organisation for the rights of the disabled.

http://www.kidstogether.org/
Information and resources that improve the quality of life for the disabled.

http://www.iod.unh.edu/projects/isd.htm
Abstracts of research on the practice of inclusion in education.

http://ep.open.ac.uk/wgma/CSIE/csiehome.html
The major UK source of information and advice on inclusive education.